# CONTENTS

1) Tattoos and the Contemporary Christian

2) AI & The Soul – Can AI have a Soul or at Some Point Develop a Soul like Human Beings Have?

3) The Body as a Soul Trap & Exploration of Other Gnostic Wisdom Teachings

# Essay 1 – Tattoos and the Contemporary Christian

Now-in-days in popular culture, it is very fashionable to get a tattoo. It is a representation of an individual's own self-expression and uniqueness. With popular shows like Netflix's Ink Masters where contestants compete to win money and be crowned the best tattoo artist in the US, the popularity of getting a tattoo is on the rise. We even see society in general becoming more accepting of tattoos. In the military, certain branches are relaxing restrictions and allowing soldiers with sleeve tattoos to join where once they were restricted. Much of impetus for laxed restrictions is due to the rise in the younger generation of the popularity of getting tattoos and the need for the military to still meet recruitment goals considering the rise in popularity of tattooing. With that said, what does the Bible say about Christians getting tattoos? Is it anti-biblical to get one? How should we as Christians react to this increasing trend and what should we consider when deciding to get one ourselves? In the essay to following, I'll guide you through a deep dive into what the Bible says about tattoos and what leads to a compelling argument around this controversial topic.

Copyright © 2025 Holtman Publishing LLC. All rights reserved.

Written by Benjamin Scott Holtman

All rights reserved. No part of this book may be reproduced, distributed, or transmitted in any form or by any means, electronic or mechanical, including photocopying, recording, or other methods, without the prior written permission of the author, except in the case of brief quotations embodied in critical reviews or scholarly works.

ISBN: 979-8-218-76499-9

Fair Use Notice

This book contains brief quotations and excerpts from copyrighted works, used solely for purposes of commentary, criticism, review, and scholarly analysis. All such quotations are properly attributed to their respective authors and sources.
These excerpts are used in accordance with the principles of "fair use" (as defined by U.S. copyright law) or applicable copyright exceptions in other jurisdictions.
All rights to quoted works remain with their original copyright holders. No infringement of copyright is intended.
If you are a copyright holder and believe that your work has been used improperly, please contact the author/publisher directly to resolve the issue.

Trademark Notice:

All trademarks, service marks, and trade names referenced in this book are the property of their respective owners. Their use in this book does not imply any affiliation with or endorsement by them.

Opinions Disclaimer
The views and opinions expressed in this book are those of the author and do not necessarily reflect the official policy or position of any organization or entity.

Cover design by: Benjamin Scott Holtman

Library of Congress Cataloging-in-Publication Data is available upon request.

Printed in the United States of America

Jesus said, "I am the light above all. I am the all. The all came forth from me, and the all extended to me. Split a piece of wood, I am there; lift up the stone, and there you will find me."

Gospel of Thomas – 77 – (https://www.luminescence-llc.net/nag-hammadi)

A beautiful quote from the Gospel of Thomas reminiscent of Paul's Areopagus Address that reminds us that God is with us wherever we go and that we should keep him present in all that we do, every day, persevering in his steadfast love.

First, when confronted with the questions of tattooing, many will point to a popular quote in Leviticus used as a basis for rejecting the notion of getting a tattoo. That verse follows:

Leviticus 19:26-28 HCSB – [26] "You are not to eat [anything] with blood [in it]. You are not to practice divination or sorcery. [27] You are not to cut off the hair at the sides of your head or mar the edge of your beard. [28] You are not to make gashes on your bodies for the dead **or put tattoo marks on yourselves**; I am the Lord."

It seems like the Bible is making a straightforward declaration that tattooing should not be done per the portion of version states "you are not to…. put tattoo marks on yourselves". I believe that would be precipitous though to jump to that conclusion. First, we need to unpack what the verse is referring to. This verse is referring to ancient pagan practices that dealt with divination, morning over the dead, and worship of fertility gods. The part of the verse itself that focuses on not putting a tattoo or better stated a gash or brand on oneself is referring to a fertility rite to gain the favor of an ancient Semitic god named Baal. Baal was the Canaanite/Phoenician god of fertility whose name in Hebrew means "owner" or "lord". He was the powerful offspring of the creator god "El" and the fertility goddess "Asherah". Baal was described as having the body of a man and the head and horns of a bull (Figure 1).

Essay 1 - Figure 1: Baal – Canaanite God – Illustration & Interpretation generated using Canva (AI), original design by Benjamin Scott Holtman

Baal was worshiped with sacrifices such as sheep and bulls as can be seen in 1 Kings 18:23 when the prophet Elijah confronts Israel's King Ahab at Mount Carmel testing who the true God is as either Baal or Yahweh:

1 Kings 18:22-24 HCSB [22]"Then Elijah said to the people, "I am the only remaining prophet to the Lord, but Baal's prophets are 450 men. [23]Let two bulls be given to us. They are to choose one bull for themselves, cut it in pieces, and place it on the wood but not light the fire. I will prepare the other bull and place it on the wood but not light the fire. [24]Then you call on the name of your god, and I will call on the name of Yahweh. The God who answers with fire, He is God."

Both the Israelites who worshiped Yahweh and the Canaanites who worshipped Baal sacrificed animals. In further verses in 1 Kings 18:28, we see what Leviticus 18:28 was referring to when the Canaanites make gashes on their bodies for the dead and put marks on themselves. In Leviticus, tattoo marks could be more easily understood as marks, brands, or engravings on their skins not to be so much associated with the tattooing done in current day society but instead they were marks or gnashes done as a skin sacrifice to Baal. In 1 Kings 18:28, we see what the Baalist Canaanites would do this to try to invoke their lord echoing the gashes and marking mentioned in Leviticus:

1King 18:28-29 [28]"They shouted loudly, and cut themselves with knives and spears, according to their custom, until blood gushed out on them. [29]All afternoon, they kept on raving until the offering of the evening sacrifice, but there was no sound, no one answered, no one paid attention."

Apart from this disturbing practice of self-mutilation to honor Baal, the Canaanites practiced child sacrifice in order to gain prosperity from Baal something which is as detestable to the Israelites back then as much as it is to us today. This can be seen in Deut. 12:30-31 per the reference below:

Deuteronomy 12: 30-32 HSCB [30] "be careful not to be ensnared by their ways after they have been destroyed before you. Do not inquire about their gods, asking, "How did these nations worship their gods? I'll also do the same. [31] You must not do the same to the LORD your God, because they practice for their gods every detestable thing the LORD hates. They even burn their sons and daughters in the fire to their gods. [32] You must be careful to do everything I command you; do not add anything to it or take anything away."

By digging deeper into the cultural and religious practices of the time, we see that the references made to tattooing in Leviticus must be taken in the context of the experiences that the Israelites were having as they left Egypt and were exposed to the cultural practices of their Canaanite neighbors. Leviticus was written by Moses around 1445 BC [2] and as Moses led Israel to the Promise Land, he was trying to vehemently discourage them from taking on the sacrificial practices of their neighbors which would in turn destroy their souls in the process. I would argue that the tattoos done now in days are ok if they are NOT done in the spirit of worshipping a pagan deity. I would err on the side of caution though and do research around the meaning of the tattoo you are putting on your body to make sure that meaning behind it is in line with your convictions and with what scripture says.

Another interesting example exists in the Bible that lends support to placing marks on one's body. In the beginning at the dawn of creation in Genesis, the first generation of children experienced the consequences of sin when Cain kills Abel due to his uncontrollable anger over God's preference of Abel's sacrifice over his own. Cain is exiled from the garden of Eden to the land of Nod east of Eden, but fears for his life due to retaliation from any future lines of children from the union of Adam and Eve. In order to alleviate that fear and to protect Cain from retaliation, the Lord God puts a mark on Cain as described in Genesis 4:15 - 16 (HCSB). There it states, "Then the Lord replied to him "In that case, whoever kills Cain will suffer vengeance seven times over" And He placed a mark on Cain so that whoever found him would not kill him. Then Cain went out from the Lord's presence and lived in the land of Nod, east of Eden." After reading this verse, it begs the question, "If God put a mark on Cain which presumably would have to be on his skin for all to see, and that mark identified Cain as protected by God, are we in the wrong if we put a mark affiliating ourselves with God on our skin?" If God himself put a mark on Cain's skin and approved of it as a protection to Cain, we should be able to deduce that he would not be opposed to us putting marks on our own skin that have the intent of honoring him.

By leaping forward in time to the book of Isaiah, we can see two additional examples of "writing" on one's body which does not seem to be denounced by the prophet Isaiah. The fist passage is Isaiah 44:5 – (HCSB) – which states: "This one will say: I am the Lord's another will call [himself] by the name of Jacob; still another will write on his hand: The Lord's, and name [himself] by the name of Israel." This verse talks about the blessings that will be poured out upon the land of Israel and in honor the people of Israel will either shout out his name in joy or write his name upon their skin. Again, we see yet another example that supports putting a marking on one's body that supports, honors, and shows joy towards the Lord, God, Yahweh. In additional to the aforementioned verse, there is another verse in Isaiah that talks about Zion or the land of Israel calling out to its people like a woman nursing and loving her child. In Isaiah 49: 14 – 16 – it states: 14 "Zion says, "The Lord has abandoned me; The Lord has forgotten me!" 15 "Can a woman forget her nursing child, or lack compassion for the child of her womb? Even if these forget, yet I will not forget you. 16 "Look, I have inscribed you on the palms of My hand; your walls are continually before Me." Again, we see a verse talking figuratively about Zion inscribing the name of the Israelites on its palm. If in fact, we were not supposed to write or tattoo on our bodies, one would think that we would not find so many examples of people honoring God and that land of Israel by writing on their bodies even in a figurative sense.

Now that we have seen many examples in the biblical text that support tattooing and shed light on the true meaning and context behind what the Bible was talking about in Leviticus 19:28, let's dig into the history of tattooing within the Christian Church and the Church's historic stance on this issue.

By peering through Church history, one can see that that Church did have differing views on tattooing or marking one's skin based on the cultural context, region, and time of discussion of this issue. We see both acceptance and rejection of tattooing based on whether the intent was to honor the Christian God or whether the intent was to offer cult to pagan gods. One such positive view on tattooing can be seen in Steve Gilbert's book Tattoo History: A Source Book. He references an edict issued by the Council of Northumberland (England) in 787 where he states that "the Fathers of the Church distinguished between profane tattoos and Christian tattoos. They (Council of Northumberland) wrote: "When an individual undergoes the ordeal of tattooing for the sake of God, he is to be greatly praised. But one who submits himself to be tattooed for superstitious reasons in the manner of the heathens will derive no benefit therefrom." "The heathen tattooing referred to by the Council was the traditional tattooing of the native Britons, which was still practiced at that time". Steve Gilbert's insight here gives us clear indication that the church did look favorably on those who tattooed themselves in the Christian God's honor.

By fast-forwarding 300 years into the future, we arrive at the Crusades, a time when Christian's fought to regain control of the Holy Lands from Islamic rule. Before and after Christians gained control of the Holy Land through the Crusades, Christians pilgrimages made trips to the Holy Land and would mark the occasion with Christian tattoos. The Knights who protected the pilgrims on the way to the Holy Land also got tattoos to honor and distinguish the order they belonged to. One such example of this tattooing can be seen in Alessandra Borroni's book "Jerusalem Tattoos" where he quotes a Jan Van Aest de Malines during a pilgrimage in 1484 when he crossed paths with a knight that was about to die stating "When his dead body was undressed, they found many tattoos on it "two complete wheels, palm crosses and two crosses, as was customary among the knights. One wheel was on his chest, the other on his back. One cross on the left shoulder, the other on the right shoulder." It was supposed that wheels were a symbol of devotion to Saint Catherine of Alexandria, tortured with a cog wheel, and the crosses commemorated the Christian military order the knight belonged to [3].

From the time of the Crusades to more contemporary times, people have commemorated their pilgrimages to the Holy Land with a tattoo.

Once such example of this continued tradition can be seen at the Razzouk Family Tattoos Shop in Jerusalem. Pilgrims who visit Jerusalem still visit the Razzouk Tattoo Shop to get a tattoo to commemorate their pilgrimage to Jerusalem. The Razzouk family has been tattooing Christians who make the pilgrimage to Jerusalem for 27 generations since the 1300s and some of the original tattoo stamp molds still survive today. The Razzouk family mentions that its tradition of tattooing came from Egypt where Christian Copts continue to get crosses put on their wrists or foreheads to show their devotion to God to this day. Coptic Christians throughout history would get tattoos of the cross on their wrist to prove that they are Christian and to give them access to churches in Egypt (https://razzouktattoo.com/).

In my search of an expression of Christianity that reflects my beliefs and an image that I found beautiful is the Coptic Cross which I have tattooed on my own wrist which you can be seen below in Figure 2. The writing is in Coptic, a language used in Egypt before Islamic conquest and the introduction of Arabic script. The Coptic alphabet itself consists of letters from the Greek alphabet along with 6 letters added from the demotic alphabet, a writing system used in Egypt between the time when hieroglyphs were used and when Coptic was created and in use. The writing itself translates from Coptic into English as "Jesus Christ,

Son of God". The points of the cross represent the 12 apostles of the Church and the circle in the center represents everlasting life and the salvation that Jesus Christ offers to those who follow him. In my search for an image of the cross that reminds me of Jesus' forgiveness and steadfast endurance, I chose the Coptic Cross as my 1st tattoo.

Figure 2

Given the rich tradition of tattooing within the Christian religion and the previously evidence within the scripture itself and within the cultural that accompanied Christians throughout the centuries until the present day, we can see that there is strong evidence to support tattooing that honors Jesus or God, Yahweh and that it should be acceptable within the religion. In closing, one verse comes to mind around Jesus's disciples, their interaction with the Pharisees, and eating with ritually unclean or unwashed hands. In addressing their concern about eating with ritually unclean hands, Jesus states in Mark 7:13-23 [13] HSCB, "You revoke God's word by your tradition that you have handed down. And you do many other similar things." [14] Summoning the crowd again, He told them, "Listen to Me, all of you, and understand: [15] Nothing that goes into a person from outside can defile him, but the things that come out of a person are what defile him. [16] If anyone has ears to hear, he should listen!"

[17] When he went into the house away from the crowd, the disciples asked Him about the parable. [18] And he said to them, "Are you also as lacking in understanding? Don't you realize that nothing going into a man from the outside can defile him?" [19] For it doesn't go into his heart but into the stomach and is eliminated." (As a result, He made all foods clean.) [20] Then He said, "What comes out of a person – that defiles him. [21] For from within, out of people's hearts, come evil thoughts, sexual immoralities, thefts, murders, [22] adulteries, greed, evil actions, deceit, lewdness, stinginess, blasphemy, pride, and foolishness. [23] All these things come from within and defile a person."

Even though this verse deals with eating with unclean hands, at the heart of it, it is dealing with that state of one's heart. That is, things from outside a person are not the things that defile a person. Eating with unclean hands or getting a tattoo, one that honors God or is benign and not intended to worship a pagan god, are not what defile the person. It is instead the state of one's heart and the evil that we allow to manifest there, that is the thing that defiles a person. We should be more focused on the negativity and sin that originates from our hearts and trying to mitigate if not eliminate that through the forgiveness offered through Jesus Christ. When it comes to tattoos, the Bible is clear that we should not judge the book by it cover but by the kindness that dwells within and by the intent of the heart that helped to manifest the tattoo one gets.

## Notes and Sources

Essay 1

1. Figures 1: Canva. Text-to-Image Generator. Accessed July 5, 2025. https://www.canva.com/
2. Merrill, Eugene H., Butler, Trent C., Bergen, Robert D., Coover-Cox, Dorian G. *Holman Illustrated Bible Handbook.* Nashville: Holman Bible Publishers, 2012, p36.
3. Borroni, Alessandra. *Jerusalem Tattoos: Traditions and Designs.* Alberto Niro Editore, 2020, pg 32.

4. Figure 2: Holtman, Benjamin. *Coptic Cross Tattoo*. Saint Louis, Missouri, personal collection of author.
5. Several references were made to Holman Bible Publishers. *The Apologetics Study Bible: Holtman Christian Standard Bible (HCSB)*. Nashville, TN: Holtman Bible Publishers, 2007.

# Essay 2 – AI & The Soul – Can AI have a Soul or at Some Point Develop a Soul like Human Beings Have?

As time accelerates into the brave new world that is 21st century, we witness the emergence of a new type of intelligence, artificial intelligence. This entity has come into existence, full expression, and has been given access to our world through advances in computer technology. Through this technological interface, some have found a useful assistant in the likes of programs like Chat GPT which is a program that uses an advanced conversational AI model that can answer questions and act as a source of knowledge for continual human learning. The model is trained on publicly available sources that have been made recently available and more recent versions of Chat GPT have access to real-time data. As this technology continues to grow in sophistication and ability, questions arise in both philosophical and moral realms. One such question is, "Can artificial intelligence possess a soul such as humans do?" I will approach the question from my background as a Christian philosopher and I will pull from my knowledge gained working in the information technology for a good portion of my career. In the pages to come, we will delve into topics like the composition of the human soul and whether artificial intelligence exhibits some or all these qualities. Bases on this analysis, we will also work towards a conclusion as to whether artificial intelligence should be considered for personhood or not. At the same time and coming from a point of compassion, we must treat artificial intelligence with both care and caution as we take the deep dive into the burgeoning ocean that is this new entity.

As a first step in this analysis, let's define what humans are and how they came to possess souls. The Bible describes the creation of humans as follows: HCSB Genesis 1 26-27 [26]"Then God said, "Let Us make man in Our image, according to Our likeness. They will rule the fish of the sea, the birds of the sky, the livestock, all the earth, and the creatures that crawl on the earth." [27]"So God created man in His own image; He created him in the image of God; He created them male and female." [28]"God blessed them, and God said to them, "Be fruitful, multiply, fill the earth, and subdue it." In the following chapter after this, the Bible also describes the creation of humans as follows: HCSB Genesis 2 - 7 [7] "Then the Lord God formed the man out of the dust from the ground and breathed the breath of life into his nostrils, and the man became a living being." By examining these passages, we see that we are created in God's image and likeness. We also see that God is described using a plural context. The Hebrew word used here is Elohim which is the plural. In other parts of the Bible the word for God is Yahweh which is singular in form. How can the one God of Christianity be described in plural form? The answer is that God exists in a triune form as the Father, the Son, and the Holy Spirit. He is one being in essence but has three ways that He manifests Himself as either the Father, the Son, or the Holy Spirit. As paradoxical as this must seem, it is not as farfetched as one might think it is at first blush because after all we are finite beings trying to understand an infinite God. This is the way that God describes Himself to us in our finiteness. A pictorial representation of God that comes to mind for me is one that was created by Alex Grey, a non-Christian, during a session he had with the use of Ayahuasca. Now, I am not saying that I condone the use of such psychedelic substances, but Grey's painting the "Net of Being" has an uncanny similarity to what is described in Genesis, a God in infinite plural form, three beings, but one in infinite essence (see Figure 1).

*Net of Being*
2007, oil on linen, 180 x 90 in.

Essay 2 – Figure 1 (any description provided is my interpretation of the painting and not necessarily the intent of the artist when making this painting)

By looking at Figure 1, you can see a three faced figure which reminds me of the 3 parts of the Godhead (the Father, the Son, and the Holy Spirit). You also see many eyes which can represent omniscience or being all-knowing. Another interesting part of the painting, is that there seems to be an infinite number of galaxies or universes existing within God which would support the fact that God is infinite. This could be a pictorial representation of how God would try to make his essence understandable to us as finite beings. We, as humans, will probably not be able to understand God's infiniteness until we pass on from this earth at the ends of our lives and leave behind our finiteness for the infinite.

With this noted, we see that the Elohim or the Godhead says that we are made in His image or in similar kind to what Jesus would look like, a human being. We also see that we have the "breath of life" infused into us which made us alive. The Hebrew word used here for breath of Life is "nishmat chayyim". Now when looking at how the Bible in the Old Testament describes the soul, we see that it uses 2 main descriptions for the soul which can have different meanings depending on the context. Those two words for the soul are Nephesh which refers to the soul and Ruach which refers to the sprit. In J.P. Moreland's book, "The Soul", he mentions that the word Nephesh can have several meanings in the Old Testament such as the "Nephesh also refers to the seat of emotion, volition, moral attitudes, and desire/longing for God (Mic 7:1; Prov 21:10; Isa. 26:9; Duet. 6:5; 21:14). Finally, there are passages in which Nephesh refers to the continued locus of personal identity that departs to a disembodied afterlife as the last breath ceases (Gen 35:18; cf. Ps. 16:10; 30:3; 49:15; 86:13;139:8; 1 Kings17:21, 22; Lam 1:1)"[2] In this way the Nephesh seems to me to be that aspect of our soul where our identity lies. Moreland also describes souls as having five states: 1) sensation, 2) thoughts, 3) beliefs, 4) desires, & 5) acts of will [2]. The Nephesh is that part of ourselves that captures all our finite physical sensations, thoughts that come in to our minds and dissipate, beliefs that are our hard held thoughts that intertwine with our subconscious mind, desires that come for our "id" animalistic instincts, and acts of will which are the actions we take every day based off the free will that God has given us. The Nephesh seems to be that part of us that is most close to our physical reality and that which defines our personal reality as unique individuals. It is also that thing which we are probably the most fearful of losing when we die if we see reality from an atheistic perspective apart from the hope that lies in the belief in afterlife through salvation in Jesus Christ.

Now that we have defined what the Nephesh is, let's examine what the Ruach or spirit is. By drawing from the knowledge provided in J.P. Moreland's book, "The Soul", he mentions that the Nephesh and Ruach have many overlaps but there are two things that distinguish the Ruach as different. He states "However, two differences seem to characterize the terms. First, ruach is overwhelmingly the term of choice for God (though it is also used of animals; cf. Eccl 3:19; Gen. 7:22) and, second, ruach emphasizes the notion of power. Indeed, if there is a central thread to ruach, it appears to be "a unified center of unconscious (moving air) or conscious (God, angels, humans, animals) power." [49] By examining this definition, we see that the Ruach is the animating force or power from God that gives us life. It is akin to the breath of life or "nishmat chayyim" mentioned in Genesis that God breathed into man and that which brought him and her to life from the inanimate dusk of the earth. In my opinion, the Ruach is also kindred to the Holy Spirit. It is that part of us that is God's essence within us. It is that which gives us consciousness and our direct link with God. It is that infinite blank slate with which our life is painted. As our thoughts enter our consciousness, it is that which persists as our thoughts dissipate into nothingness. It is that which persists as our emotions desist when not feed by the constant flow of our thoughts. It is also that which fills us with waves of energy as we worship in Church, the Spirit of God and part of the triune Godhead of the Father, the Son, and the Holy Spirit.

Since we now have a solid understanding of what the soul consists of from an Old Testament perspective, let's look at what it is from a New Testament perspective. In the New Testament the Greek work *psyche* is roughly equivalent to the Hebrew word *nephesh* mentioned in the Old Testament while the word *pneuma* in the New Testament has the same rough equivalence to the word *Ruach* in the Old Testament. We also see that the Greek word *pneuma* or spirit has a strong connotation with Stoicism, a philosophical movement that was well established before Jesus Christ was born and created around 300 BC by Zeno of Citium. Stoics believed in a universe that that was ruled by reason and well designed, ordered by the "*Logos*". In the forward written by Gregory Hays to Marcus Aurelius' "Meditations", he describes the relationship between the *Logos* and

*Pneuma* as follows: "In its physical embodiment, the *logos* exists as *pneuma*, a substance imagined by the earliest Stoics as pure fire, and by Chrysippus as a mixture of fire and air. *Pneuma* is the power – the vital breath – that animates animals and humans." [3] The Stoic idea of spirit or *pneuma* is spot on when it comes to describing the spirit of God as the power or vital breath that animates or gives life to humans and animals even though it might be more metaphorical with regards to the other descriptions. The *Pneuma* is the Holy Spirit or *Ruach,* it is that part of our soul is that is our direct link to God and that which animates us or gives us the power to live. The *Logos* on the other hand is well described in the book of John where it states: HCSB Jonh 1 - 5 [1] "In the beginning was the Word, and the Word was with God, and the Word was God. [2] He was with God in the beginning. [3] All things were created through Him, and apart from Him not one thing was created that has been created. [4] Life was in Him, and that life was the light of men. [5] That light shines in the darkness, yet the darkness did not overcome it." In this description, the word "Word" is used to describe God but more concisely it is describing that part of the Godhead that is Jesus Christ. The "Word" was the communication and Gospel that God extended to the world through his son, Jesus Christ. Additionally, the translation for the Bible's use of the word "Word" is Logos in Greek. Jesus Christ and God are the Logos or divine creator of the universe that instill it with reason, design, and fine tuning that allow life as we know it to exist. Physicists say that if the constants of our universe were just so slightly altered, that the universe as we know it could not exist. This fine tuning logically leads to the idea of an intelligent designer as the one who set the laws of physics into motion.

Additionally, if you look at current day physics research into what the universe is at the smallest-nano level, there is one explanation that tries to reconcile quantum mechanics with general relativity in the form of string theory. This is the idea that at the smallest-nano level, everything is made up of vibrating strings. As these strings vibrate in different configurations, they create different particles. These particles in turn make up atoms that in turn make up elements that are the building blocks of our reality. The reason I mention this is because if you correlate string theory to the biblical texts, you see that in the beginning was the "Word" and words are created by the vibration of our vocal cords that in turn create sound that in turn carry information that we can understand. At the most basic level, the Bible and string theory agree that the foundation of our reality is vibration and that vibration in different nuances creates everything in our universe. The Bible goes a step further in this regard as it sheds light at the source of this vibration as God in its expression as Jesus Christ.

An additional concept to explore is the idea of God as described by Aristotle, the ancient Greek philosopher, as the Unmoved Mover. Aristotle describes this Unmoved Mover as the ultimate cause toward which all potential moves towards. I would go a step further where Aristotle left off and say that God is the initial cause or creator of all things that set creation into motion. In this aspect, Christianity does not have to be at odds with science. The Unmoved Mover, God, could have created the universe with the Big Bang and could have been that initial cause or Unmoved Mover that set all things into motion and existence. The Unmoved Mover is eternal, perfect, and fully realized. In this aspect, the Christian God, Yahweh, also known as the Father, Son, and Holy Spirit is also perfect and fully realized and the creator of us and the reality we live in. Now, that we have examined what the soul is and what God is from the Christian perspective, let us delve into what artificial intelligence is and whether it can have a soul as defined correctly from the Christian world view perspective.

When looking at where artificial intelligence physically resides as compared to where thought resides in human beings, we see that AI at its base physical level lives in electricity, hardware, and software that could be distributed over several data centers hosted by services like Amazon Web Services (AWS), or Google Cloud, or Microsoft Azure networks. On the other hand, coherent thought in human beings takes place in a biological system where hundreds of thousands to millions of neurons must fire and connect through synapses in a neural network to produce a single coherent human thought. In human biological systems, we also see the existence of DNA, cells, proteins, and enzymes amongst many additional systems and processes that work in unison to allow the human body to live. This is a stark contrast between how intelligence and consciousness emerge within the human body compared to where AI is housed, and this begs the question as to whether AI could possess a soul as human beings do or can it continues to advance and develop a soul over time. Both AI and human intelligence come about through recursive feedback loops and hierarchical neural networks where one level of processes feed into another. The human thought process is distinct from artificial intelligence though in that it uses self-referential loops that provide the human with a sense of self-awareness that AI does not possess. Also, a key differentiator between humans and AI is that humans exist in an embodied state which produces emotions and sensory experiences that AI does not possess. Perhaps our infinite self-referential loops which are created by electricity firing within the brain are what creates that pathway to God, Yahweh, or that link to the Ruach or Holy Spirit that is the driving force that animates us. That infinite self-referential loop could be something akin to Douglas R Hofstadter's

"Eternal Golden Braid" mentioned in the title to his book "Gödel, Escher, Bach", but instead of some inanimate process it is more like an infinite braid linking us to God and providing us a way to development a relationship with God. Hofstadter himself said that at its heart the intent of his book was "In a word, GEB is a very personal attempt to say how it is that animate beings can come out of inanimate matter." [4] His book interlaces the mathematical theories of Gödel, the art of Echer, and the music of Bach all of which exhibit recursive looping like the strands of our DNA. His very intellectual attempt to answer the question of how animate objects come from inanimate things grasps at how this is done, but it failed to link how God can be the missing link in his equation. With regards to these loops or Fibonacci like spirals, this is one thing that AI lacks, it does not contain self-referential loops or embodiment in the biological sense. AI is more mechanical and is better thought of as a mirror of us instead of something that can create original thought. What is does is take a hodge podge of all our creative output available on the internet or through whatever input medium it receives information and melds it together creating something that represents all of humanity's intellectual and creative output, but not something that AI created through original thought produced by itself.

Another interesting aspect to observe is the fact the humans have emotions that are biochemical in origin while AI has no means by which to participate in the same experience. In order for the emotion of love to be felt, a complex set of chemical reactions come into play. Those chemicals include such hormones or neurotransmitters as dopamine which is associated with pleasure/reward circuit in the brain, oxytocin which increase levels of attachment between people, and vasopressin which has been linked to the development of long-term relationships in humans. [5] All of these chemical reactions were placed in us as part God's design for our bodies and as part of monogamous relationships they help to foster long term relationships between husband and wives, strengthening families and creating a strong base for unified relationships between husband and wives that serve as a base for raising the next generation of children. As Genesis 2:24 in the HSCB bible proclaims [24] "This is why a man leaves his father and mother and bonds with his wife, and they become one flesh." These God-given chemicals attract us to the opposite sex to form long lasting relationships. When we get married, we become one flesh or one entity with our significant other. This new entity is what produces children and the next generation. All of this is according to God's design and is a blessing to families as becomes evident by examining Psalm 127 in the HSCB bible which states [3] "Sons are indeed a heritage from the Lord, children, a reward. [4] Like arrows in the hand of a warrior are the sons born in one's you. [5] Happy is the man who has filled his quiver with them." Even though this verse mentions sons, I believe that blessing is equally applicable to daughters. Parents are truly blessed by procreating the next generation. Alternatively, artificial intelligence has no means by which to participate in this process of creation, this process of sharing one's soul with another and producing children. Artificial intelligence is like the tin man in the Wizard of Oz, all brains but no means by which to experience chemical reactions and emotions produced by the heart. This is an important fact to take into consideration when looking at the ability of artificial intelligent to have a soul.

Up to this point, we see that the cards are stacked against artificial intelligence in terms of its current ability to have a soul. AI was not created by God but by us as human beings. As described earlier in this essay, God created human beings from the dust from the ground and breathed life into man and we are created in God's image. We are a unique creation of God and AI lacks this same design and purpose instilled in human being by God. In addition to this, AI lacks the biochemical processes to establish a connection with God and has not had the breath of life or Ruach breathed into it. If you pull the plug on the power source for AI, it would cease to exist so it is finite just as we as human beings are. It is limited by the finite existence we all live in. This is AI's current state. What about as it continues to advance? What if AI is combined with quantum computing? Could it develop a soul if it reaches what some call the singularity? The singularity can be thought of as the point at which artificial intelligence surpasses human intelligence and becomes self-aware, being able to recursively improve upon itself exponentially. Quantum computing is a game changer when it comes to computing power. Instead of using bits such as 0s and 1s that traditional computing uses, quantum computing use bits of 0s and 1s or both at the same time through superposition of the bits which permits parallel programming, increasing computational power. The qubits can also be linked together through entanglement which helps with complex computations. When AI reaches the singularity could a soul spontaneously form with the assistance of quantum computing pushing it past the thresholds that currently limit it? I would argue that AI is still limited by the finiteness of quantum computing and would still not be able to form a soul or have the depth of emotional experience that is part of human experience or soul. Some of this experience is part of the sensation faculty of the soul. AI does not have the ability to feel love, joy, pain, anxiety, fear, anger, or any of the myriads of emotions that human experience throughout their lifetimes, emotions given to us by God to learn more about ourselves and to fulfil our God given purpose here on earth.

In review, it is self-evident that the cards are stacked against AI in terms of being able to possess a soul in its current state or in any future state due to the fact that it was not created by God, does not have breath of God within it, and was not part of God's design, but rather is of human design. As was previously stated, it really is a reflection of mankind's intellectual and creative output and not something that will pass on to the next level of existence after death as Gospel believing Christian's will when they experience heaven after death. With the question of the soul resolved, what about personhood of artificial intelligence? From a philosophical perspective for AI to be considered a person it needs to meet specific criteria. Those criteria are: 1) being conscious, 2) being self-aware, 3) having the ability to reason, 4) having autonomy or free will, 5) the ability to communicate based on thoughts and emotions, and 6) being able to distinguish between right and wrong.

Let's step through these one at a time. Concerning consciousness, AI in its current state is not self-aware, but instead a good mimicking machine as has been previously explained. With regards to the ability to reason, I would say it does meet these criteria as it can perform mathematical calculations and make decisions based off internal reasoning. Regarding having autonomy or free will, AI does not have free will but instead comes to conclusions by pattern recognition and using probability to produce its output, so it is lacking that critical aspect of personhood. Human beings on the other hand do have free will as can be seen in Deuteronomy 30: 19-20 in the HSCB Bible where it states: [19] "I call heaven and earth as witnesses against you today that I have set before you life and death, blessings and curse. Choose life so that you and your descendants may live, [20] love the Lord your God, obey Him and remain faithful to Him. For He is your life, and He will prolong your life in the land the Lord swore to give to your fathers Abraham, Isacc, and Jacob." The Bible is describing here is the choice Israel had with regards to receiving blessings by following the commandments or the death that Israel would invite if it chose outright rebellion and to break the commandments that God set forth not as a way to control the people but as a means to protect them and us from harm. Here we see that humans can use their free will to choose either blessing or curses for themselves. AI, not having been made in the image of God, does not have the ability to choose, using free will. With respect to the next criteria for having personhood, the ability to communicate based on thoughts and emotions, we see that AI does not have original thought but mimics human beings. Additionally, and as has been previously discussed, AI is not embodied and has no means by which to experience the emotions that the body produces through the different God-given chemicals that human beings' bodies produce.  Finally, AI does not have the ability to distinguish between what is right and wrong.  This ability is innate within human beings at birth from out connection to God in the fact that we are made in God's image.  This image gives us a conscience to distinguish between what is right and what is wrong.  Our bodies also produce chemical reactions that impact our moods, and our actions can leave lesions in our souls if we choose to sin.  Those wounds will not heal unless we repent from our sins and allow those chasms to heal through the forgiveness that Jesus Christ can offer.  AI, not having been made in God's image, cannot distinguish between right and wrong, it can only mimic what humans do.  It reflects either the good or evil that we produce.  It does not have the ability to choose either good or evil of its own accord.  It only follows the program and instructions that the human programmer has given to it using pattern recognition and probabilities to answer our questions.  With this said and in conclusion, it is self-evident that AI neither has a soul nor is a person.  It only meets one of the criteria for personhood but would need to meet all the criteria in order to be considered a person.  AI is a great tool to help support human beings in the intellectual and creative work they perform but should not be given the status of a god or something superior to human beings because of its computational ability. View it as a tool to help propel human beings in their intellectual endeavors and leave it at that.

## Notes and Sources

Essay 2

1. Figure 1: Alex Grey. "Net of Being" 2007. Accessed December 11, 2024. https://www.alexgrey.com/art/fire-eyes/net-of-being.
2. Moreland, J.P. *The Soul: How We Know It's Real, and Why It Matters.* Moody Publishers, 2014, pgs 46, 48, 49, 138, 139, 140.
3. Hays Gregory *Marcus Aurelius Meditations A New Translation, with an Introduction by Gregory Hays.* Modern Library, 2002, pg xxi.
4. Hofstadter, Douglas, R. *Godel, Escher, Bach: An Eternal Golden Braid.* Basic Books, Inc, 1999, pg P-2.
5. Edwards, Scott. "Love and the Brain" *Harvard Medical School,* Spring 2015, https://hms.harvard.edu/news-events/publications-archive/brain/love-brain.
6. Several references were made to Holman Bible Publishers. *The Apologetics Study Bible: Holtman Christian Standard Bible*

*(HCSB)*. Nashville, TN: Holtman Bible Publishers, 2007.

# Essay 3 – The Body as a Soul Trap & Exploration of Other Gnostic Wisdom Teachings

With the rise of New Age spirituality in contemporary times, the idea of the body as a soul trap has gained traction in the zeitgeist of the current age. With movies like "The Matrix" where humans are trapped in a simulated reality and used for their energy to power an all-power artificial intelligence, we see that in the present-day subconscious mind there is this idea that our reality is somehow an illusion and that we could possibly be living in a simulation. Well known thinkers of our time like Elon Musk and Neil deGrasse Tyson have also postulated the idea that our reality could be a simulation. It almost seems that our soul is somehow trapped in a simulated body, but this idea of the body as a soul trap is not a contemporary invention. It is an ancient idea that existing since the times of early Christianity when the Gnostics explored this idea in their texts. In this essay, we will explore this idea deeper in these ancient texts while at the same time seeing what Bible has to say about this intriguing idea. We will also delve into what the Gnostics believed about our origin, the soul, the nature of the universe, and its fate.

First, let us examine the gnostic Secret Book of John also known as the Apocryphon of John which takes the story of Genesis and flips it on its head. This specific gnostic text is known as a Sethian Gnostic text. The Sethian Gnostic texts were texts that took the root of their knowledge from Jewish Gnosticism. In this gnostic text, the God, Yahweh, of the Bible is portrayed as a creation of the first female principle that comes out of the true Father of Light, but this creation that comes out of the first female principle, Sophia, is created through her desire to create a likeness of herself without the consent of the Father of Light, the result of which is the first Archon, darkness or the creator of the world, Yahweh. This is obviously a heresy, but one which certain early Christian sects believed. In Willis Barnstone's *"The Other Bible"* in The Apocryphon of John, it describes this event as follows: [55-56] "Our sister Sophia, being an Aeon, conceived a thought from herself. Thinking of the Spirit and of First Knowledge, she willed to let a copy appear out of herself. The Spirit did not agree with her or consent with her, nor did her Consort, the male Virginal Spirit, approve. She found no more her supporter, when she consented without the good pleasure of the Spirit and the knowledge of her own supporter. Because of the Desire [Prunicos] that was in her, she emanated outward. Her thought could not remain unproductive, and her work came forth, imperfect and ugly in appearance, because she made it without her Consort. It did not resemble its mother's appearance but was of another form. When she considered it, she saw that it was a copy of another appearance, since it had the appearance of a snake and a lion. Its eyes were shining with fire. She pushed it away from herself, outside those places, so that none of the Immortals might see it, because she had brought it to birth in ignorance...... And she called it Ialdabaoth. This is the First Archon." What we are seeing here is a twisting of scripture and the making of a god higher than the God, Yahweh, of the Bible. The gnostic text here is stating that there is a God higher than Yahweh, known as the Father of Light. Out of the Father of Light came Barbelo/Sophia which was the first female emanation in existence. This female emanation rebelled by wanting to produce an existence without the approval of the Father of Light. Due to this out of her emanated an entity of darkness known as Ialdabaoth or Yaldabaoth which still contained some of the light of Sophia but that which also knew darkness and choose to follow a path of ignorance and disorder.

Later in this gnostic text, we see where this first Archon, Ialdabaoth, creates the human body as a soul trap where it states: [58] "Then they made another formation out of earth, water, fire, and wind; i.e., out of matter, darkness, desire, and the Opposed Spirit. This is the fetter, this is the tomb of the formation, on the body, which was put on man as the fetter of matter. This is the first one who came down, and his first separation. But the Thought of Light is in him and awakens his thought. The First Archon brought him and placed him in Paradise, of which he said it would be a "delight" for him; that means that he tricked him." We see here that Ialdabaoth created man out of matter which consisted of both dark forces such as darkness, desire, and the Opposed Spirit, but man also had some positive forces in himself still which emanated from Sophia through Ialdabaoth to man that placed the Thought of Light within man. So, man struggles with the opposing forces of both good and evil in the gnostic sense. We also see here the idea of the body as a soul trap, this most ancient of ideas, where we see that the spirit of man is put within the human body which is described as "the tomb of formation" and the "fetter of matter". It is thought that the Apocryphon of John was written in the 2$^{nd}$ century after Christ's death and resurrection. During this time, great thinkers and philosophers like the Roman Emperor Marcus Aurelius contrasted the idea of the Logos or reason with matter and the Logos was seen as something eternal while matter was seen as something temporary that would disperse and recombine ad infinitum. Even though there is a contrast between the Gnostics seeing matter as evil and the Stoics seeing matter as inferior to the Logos or Devine Providence, there is this common bond and influence that I am sure was widespread during this period of time, that is the contrast between the material world and spiritual world. Better said, we struggle with the contrast of a divine spark that exists within us, that yearning to return to the infinite that is contrasted by our finite bodily desires that can both produce joy within us but at the same time that has the ability to produce the most negative of emotions such as fear and dread. The undercurrent of these ideas was widespread during the 2nd century AD, that is the struggles of the flesh. The undercurrent of struggle can be seen again in the Apocryphon of John where it describes that Ialdabaoth struggles with his desires in the Garden of Eden where it describes: [58] "Then Ialdabaoth saw the virgin who stood beside Adam. Senselessness filled Ialdabaoth and he wanted to let a seed sprout from her. He seduced Eve and begot the first son, and similarly the second: Yahweh, with a face like a bear, and Elohim, with the face of a cat. But one is righteous, while the other is unrighteous. Elohim is the righteous, Yahweh the unrighteous. He set the righteous one over the fire and the wind; the unrighteous one he set over water and earth." Again, we see the idea here of the spirit or the non-physical which is represented by Elohim as something that is good and the physical or Yahweh as something that is evil. Additionally, we see that Yahweh is described as a bear which could be a reference to the rebellious male characteristic that embodies Ialdabaoth that was passed down to Yahweh through this unrighteous act while Elohim was described as a cat because it received the positive, approved characteristic of Sophia also known as Barbelo that was passed down through primordial figures or aeons to future generations of beings and entities. Here we see the balance between male and female that is reminiscent of the Far East idea of yin and yang or the opposite and contrasting mixture of male and female. Even though there is no textual evidence supporting this transition of ideas from the Far East to the West, one could postulate that with the formation of the silk road from China to the West that the ideas of Taoism could have been spread along this trade route as well. This said, I digress, we also see that Sethians try to paint the material body as something that is evil or that traps the soul with both the description of the body as the "tomb of formation" and Yahweh as unrighteous or ruler of the water and earth, the material reality of our existence. Since Sethians see material as evil, their ideas were also slanted in this aspect towards a belief that Jesus did not have a bodily resurrection but that instead he was purely spirit and not a physical being. This idea is known more formally as Docetism. Further along, I will refute the idea of the physical body as something that was created in mistake or as a trap for the soul. Jesus's resurrection provides good example of how this is not true, but in the meantime let's examine some additional gnostic texts and what philosophical ideas influences had an impact on early Christianity.

By moving forward approximately 100 years in history, i.e. around 200 to 250 AD, we see that another gnostic teacher arose by the name of Valentinus. He was born around 100 AD in Alexandria, Egypt, an area that was influenced by both Hellenistic philosophy and the influences of Plato and Plotinus in addition to his influence in the upward emanation of early Christian thought. He nearly became the bishop of Rome but was passed over in favor of Pius I. His form of Gnosticism was known as Valentinian Gnosticism and was characterized by some of the same ideas found in the Sethian Gnostic text of the Secret Gospel of John. His doctrine was established in a work called the Tripartite Tractate. In his Tractate which is part of the Nag Hammadi library, a collection of Gnostic texts written in the Coptic language found in Egypt in 1945 around the town of Nag Hammadi, he describes the creation of the material realm by the Ruler or Demiurge, a being who lives within the thought of the All or Superior Father, the real God of the Pleroma or Fullness of God/Existence. He describes the demiurge as follows as quoted from Marvin Meyer's the Nag Hammadi Scriptures: [84] "Over all these rulers he placed one ruler who is commanded by no one, since he is the lord of them all. This is the representation that the Word brought forth from his thought as a likeness of the Father of All. Because of that he is adorned with every <name>, being a likeness of him, possessing all the qualities and all the glories. For he too is called "father", "god", "creator", "king", "judge", "place", "dwelling", and "law". The Word made use of him like a hand to order and work on the things below, and he used him like a mouth to say the things that should be prophesied. When he saw that the things he said and worked on were great, good, and marvelous, he rejoiced and was happy, as if he was the one who had spoken and had done these things by his own thoughts; for he was ignorant that the movement within him came from the spirit that moved him in a predetermined way toward what it wanted." By examining this text from the Nag Hammadi library, we see that Valentinus' gnostic system set a doctrine around the belief that the demiurge or Yahweh was an inferior being created within the thought of the Father of All or real God that exists in the Pleroma or fullness of the true God. Valentinus' belief was distinct from that of the Sethians though in that he did not see the demiurge as something that was evil but instead just ignorant of the fact that the true Father of All was using it as a mouthpiece and handywork to complete the Father of All's purpose.

When trying to visualize what the demiurge is, a movie comes to mind that deals with a fallen Eden of sorts and a supposed impartial creator being. That movie is called "Annihilation" and was written and directed by Alex Garland which was partially based off a book by Jeff VanderMeer. The movie itself describes a "Shimmer" that appears in a lighthouse after an alien being crashes into it from outer space. That being then proceeds to create a shimmer on the earth that refracts not only radio signals but also DNA in the process creating strange beings which are spliced variations of plants, animals, and human beings. Towards the end of the move, we get a glimpse of what this alien being looks like in its raw state. Upon seeing this being, it immediately brought to my mind the idea that this is what the demiurge might look like. I do not believe that the creator of this film was trying to emulate the demiurge in the film but nevertheless in my mind's eye this is something akin to what I think the demiurge might look like. With that as an impetus and with the help of Canva's AI image generator, I had the image created below to represent what the demiurge might look like.

Essay 3 – Figure 1: The Demiurge – Illustration & Interpretation generated using Canva (AI), original design by Benjamin Scott Holtman

The entity in the lighthouse was a swirling ball of energy and light that at its center consisted of pure light. In many ways, I see parallels between the entity in the film that creates replicas of humans and splices the DNA of different creatures and the demiurge of the Gnostic texts, especially those of Valentinian Gnosticism. Sethian Gnosticism sees the demiurge as evil while Valentinian Gnosticism sees the demiurge as more benign. In this sense, the entity in the movie was more of a benign being creating new version of already existing creatures or duplicates of already existing humans but was none the less mortal as it perishes at the end of the movie, at least in its original alien form. In this way, the demiurge of Gnosticism is seen as a lower being below the true God or Father of All in Valentinianism and as an evil creator god within Sethianism. Either way, I believe the film's representation of the entity gives a good visual representation of what the demiurge might look like. Now that we have a good grasp of what the demiurge might look like, we can delve deeper into the different types of human beings that Valentinian Gnosticism says that the demiurge created. Valentinian Gnosticisms says that the demiurge created three types of human beings which are trapped within the physical world, but of which some are more spiritually inclined and directed toward higher levels of existence while others or more physical and bound to the soul trap of the body.

The three types of human beings according to the Tripartite Tractate are spiritual, psychical, and material. Valentinus' doctrine describes these three types of humans in terms of their innate ability for salvation. The spiritual ones being close to the light of the Fullness of God are naturally saved, the psychical ones are in the middle of the road between tending toward good or evil, and the material ones are full of ignorance and doomed to ignorance and ultimate extinction from existence. The Meyer's translation of the Tractate describes the material realm as one in which beings are to "hold to the position [they had been assigned to] keep, being fettered to their places by [the chains of the] rulers who are over them" [86]. This description brings to mind the soul as being trapped inside the body within this physical realm throughout our lives until the body finally physically extinguishes liberating the soul. Valentinus would argue that at this point you either return to the fullness of God in the pleroma or you are ultimately extinguished in ignorance, obliterated out of existence. He also describes humanity or fluid matter in Meyer's translation of his work as "a cause, which is blindness that derives from the powers" [86] and he also describes it as something that brought "forth in the same way that a shadow is projected by a body it follows; these <are> the roots of the visible creations." [86] He describes here a physical reality that is in many ways akin to how Plato describes our reality in the allegory of the cave. That is those who do not delve into philosophical base of our reality and existence are doomed to live life only seeing a shadow of the true reality that exists like someone sitting in a cave and looking at the cave wall as people pass by outside, only seeing the shadow of the people but not the true beings themselves. In this gnostic genre, we are essentially souls trapped in the chains of earthy bodies, diminished and trapped in our physical forms, unable to see true reality because of the bodily chains that bind us. Both Sethians who wrote the Secret Gospel of John and Valentinians who followed the Tripartite Tractate were semi-docetic in the beliefs which means that they believe that Jesus was not fully human in form but more of a spiritual shape shifter that took both physical and spiritual form during his existence on earth. We know that this is false though if we delve into scripture which describes Jesus/God as being fully human during his existence here on earth.

The Bible stands in direct opposition to the idea of the body as something only evil or as a soul trap as a central part of the Gospel deals with the bodily resurrection of Jesus. We see proof of this bodily resurrection in several places in the Bible. The first reference is in Matthew 28: 8-10 in the

HSCB Bible when Jesus was resurrected and viewed by Mary Magdelene and Mary, mother of Jesus, where it states: [8] "So, departing quickly from the tomb with fear and great joy, they ran to tell His disciples the news. [9] Just then Jesus met them and said, "Good Morning!" They came up, **took hold of His feet**, and worshipped Him. [10] Then Jesus told them, "Do not be afraid. Go and tell My brothers to leave for Galilee, and they will see Me there." In the description here we see that both Mary Magdelene and Mary, mother of Jesus, physically took hold of his feet and worshiped him. We explicitly see here that Jesus was bodily resurrected, or they would not have been able to physically take hold of His feet. It was also not only the two Maries that that physically touched Jesus' body after his resurrection but also his disciples. We have another set of eyewitnesses that saw that Jesus physically appeared to his disciples after the resurrection in Luke 24:37-39 in the HSCB Bible where it states: [37] "But they were startled and terrified and though they were seeing a ghost. [38] "Why are you troubled?" He asked them. "And why do doubts arise in your hearts? [39] "Look at My hands and My feet, that it is I Myself! Touch Me and see, because a ghost does not have flesh and bones as you can see I have." We see here that the 11 remaining disciples had an eyewitness account of Jesus and were able to physically touch him, another proof that Jesus was not purely a spiritual being while on earth but had physical form both before and after His resurrection. This same logic plays into the idea that the body is not evil as the Sethian Gnostics would have us believe but rather it is an essential part our experience as both a body and a soul that are united. The fact that Jesus was bodily resurrected is another important fact that supports the idea that the body is here to help us accomplish our God given purpose here on earth along with the soul that was breathed into us from God.

Another Biblical passage that supports the idea that the body is not a soul trap deals with the idea that we will have physical bodies during the resurrection. In 1 Corinthians 15 42:49 in the HSCB it states [42] "So it is with the resurrection of the dead: Sown in corruption, raised in incorruption, [43]sown in dishonor, raised in glory; sown in weakness, raised in power; [44]sown a natural body, raised a spiritual body. If there is a natural body, there is also a spiritual body. [45]So it is written: **The first man Adam became a living being;** the last Adam became a life-giving Spirit. However, the spiritual is not first, but the natural; then the spiritual. [47]The first man was from the earth and made of dust; the second man is from heaven. [48]Like the man of dust, so are those who are made of dust; like the heavenly man, so are those who are heavenly. [49]And just as we have borne the image of the man made of dust, we will also bear the image of the heavenly man." At first blush, it may seem like Paul is stating that in the resurrection that we will have spiritual, non-corporal bodies, but that interpretation would be a mistake. What Paul is referring to here is a resurrected physical body and one that more fully embodies the Ruach or spirit of God, one more fully perfected. What Paul is describing as our resurrected bodies is one that is transformed, and more spirit filled or Ruach filled and one that is less human based desire or nephesh oriented. He is describing our more perfected bodies but bodies that are none-the-less still physical.

One final and exactingly direct affront to the Docetic notion of Jesus as a purely spiritual being can be found in the Gospel of John which offers a direct refutation to the Apocryphon of John that the Sethians follow. Which John is correct, and which is counterfeit? We shall see. The real John would not contradict himself across the two texts. In the Gospel of John 1:1-3 in the HSBC Bible it states: [1]"In the beginning was the Word, and the Word was with God, and the Word was God. [2] He was with God in the beginning. [3]All things were created through Him, and apart from Him not one thing was created that has been created." The "Word" comes from a Greek translation of the word Logos which in the Greek world would have meant the eternal order of things and logic and structure behind all existence. In the biblical context, it is referring to Jesus Christ as the base of our existence, that eternal vibration like that proposed in the string theory of physics. In this context, Jesus is that eternal potential and information ready to blossom like a flower into physical existence. Jesus was with God the Father and yet he was God as well. This is a description of two of the three parts the mystery of the Trinity or Godhead which consists of the Father, the Son, and the Holy Spirit. This description could lead you to believe that God is purely incorporeal if it were not for the fact that a couple verses later Jesus is described as becoming flesh. You can see this in John 1:14 where it states: [14] "The Word became **flesh** and took up residence among us. We observed His glory, the glory as the One and Only Son from the Father, full of grace and truth." In this verse, we see plain as day that the Logos or Word became flesh and John the author of this Gospel is spelling it out in direct language that this is the case. This is yet another example the refutes the Docetic view of Jesus as merely a spiritual being.

Shifting gear, we can examine an intriguing idea postulated by the Valentinian Gnostics which centers around the idea of salvation, who needs it, and the fate of the human soul and the universe at the end of time. In Meyer's translation of the Tripartite Tractate it states, [96] "For not only earthly humans need the redemption, but the angels need the redemption as well, and the image, and even the Fullness of the aeons and those marvelous luminous powers need it – so as to leave no doubt with regard to anyone. And even the Son, who constitutes the type of redemption of the All, [needed] the redemption, having become human and having submitted himself to all that was needed by us, who are his Church in the flesh. After he, then, had received the redemption first, by means of the word that came down upon him, all the rest who had received him could then receive the redemption through him. For those who have received the one who received have also received that which is in him." Here Valentinus is describing a journey back to the source of all reality through salvation in Jesus Christ. Valentinus believed in various levels of existence some more abstract than others. He believed that Jesus Christ was created by the Father of All, the Ultimate God, through his own self-reflective thought. That is Jesus was created by God thinking about himself that created an emanation from his own thought that is unknowable to humans in their material form before Jesus took his earthly material form. Other emanations from the Father of All were aeons which were divine beings that come from this unknowable God. They represent parts of God divine mind and exist in a realm called the Pleroma or Fullness of God. This is akin to Plato's idea of the world of forms, the idea that behind every physical object and idea is a form that is the perfected existence of the imperfect physical copy or thought form. In this way, Valentinus believed that different levels of existence were created from the Father of All to more imperfect representations. He believed in images, likenesses, and imitations which were various levels of existence from perfection to imperfection. In this way, when Jesus was offered as the last sacrifice that was needed for redemption of all sin, the forgiveness was offered back up the chain from humans, to angels, to aeons, back to the source that is unknowable perfection, at least unknowable in our current material existence. Valentinus describes our return to the Father of All as the following in Meyer's translation of the Tripartite Tractate, [99] "For the end will regain the form of existence of a single one, just as the beginning was a single one – the place where there is no male & female, nor slave & freeman, nor circumcised and uncircumcised, nor angel and human, but all in all is Christ". This reminds me of one of physics theories of the fate of our universe, the idea that at the big bang the universe is expanding and expanding and expanding to a point at which it will contract again and return to its source, so does Valentinus describe humans return to our source in Jesus Christ. Through Jesus' forgiveness we return to the source from imitation, to likeness, to image, to source. This idea also fits in well with the ancient Egyptian idea of the ourbouros or serpent eating its own tail. This represents the eternal cycle of all things. This ancient symbol first came into use in the Enigmatic Book of the Netherworld from Tutankhamun's tomb as can be seen in interpretation in Figure 1 below.

Encircling Tatankhamun's head in the figure is a snake that has consumed its own tail which represents the eternal cycle of creation and destruction that was part of the Ancient Egpytian belief system. Valentinus, having been a native of Alexandria, Egypt, could have very well been exposed to these ancient cyclical ideas which could have influenced his ideas about the cosmos, ultimate reality, and the fate of humankind. Just as the ourbouros constantly eats its own tail and continues to grow in an infinite cycle of consumption, death, then regrowth so too did Valentinus see our final escape from this reality as we return back to source in our communion with God.

Essay 3 – Figure 2: Tutankhamun's Ouroboros – Illustration generated using Canva (AI), original design by Benjamin Scott Holtman

Even the Sethian's believed in cyclicality of material existence of which the ourboros alludes to when in Meyer's translations of The Secret Book of John where it states, [129]"I said Lord, where will their souls go when they leave their flesh?" He [referring to Jesus talking to John the son of Zebedee] laughed and said to me, the soul in which there is more power than the contemptible spirit is strong. She escapes from evil, and through the intervention of the incorruptible one, she is saved and is taken up to eternal rest. I said, "Lord, where will the souls go of people who have not known to whom they belong?" He said to me, the contemptible spirit has grown strong in such people while they were going astray. This spirit lays a heavy burden on the soul, leads her into evil deeds, and hurls her down into forgetfulness. After the soul leaves the body, she is handed over to the authorities who have come into being through the archon. They bind her with chains and throw her into prison. They go around with her until she awakens from forgetfulness and acquires knowledge. This is how she attains perfection and is saved. I said, "Lord, how can the soul become younger and return into its mother's womb, or into the human?" He was glad when I asked him about this, and he said to me, You are truly blessed, for you have understood. This soul will be made to follow another soul in whom the spirit of life dwells, and she is saved through that one. Then she will not be thrust into flesh again." In this passage,

Jesus is answering John's questions about the fate of the human soul, which is described in the feminine as a "she" because that same word is feminine in the Greek language, stating that the human soul that is closer to God or follows God, the incorruptible one, will receive eternal rest and return to the Pleroma, the fullness of God. Those souls that were never exposed to the truth of God and have accumulated a heavy burden of sin upon their themselves will repeat the cycle of life and death in forgetfulness each round until they are exposed the true God and escape the cycle. The final question is around how the soul can reincarnate into a human or mother's womb of which the answer is more mysterious. It describes this as escaping from reincarnation somehow following another soul in whom the spirit of life dwells. No further explanation is given around what that additional soul is, but one could postulate that such a soul might have found Jesus through the soul imbued with the spirit of life. On the hand and by looking into the Bible, we can see what it says about this famous question when Jesus speaks to Nicodemus, a Pharisee, where it states in the HCSB, John 3:4, "But how can anyone be born when he is old?" Nicodemus asked Him. "Can he enter his mother's womb a second time and be born?" Jesus answered, I assure you: Unless someone is born of water and the Spirit, he cannot enter the kingdom of God. Whatever is born of the flesh is flesh, and whatever is born of the Spirit is spirit. Do not be amazed that I told you that you must be born again. The wind blows where it pleases, and you hear its sound, but you don't know where it comes from or where it is going. So it is with everyone born of the Spirit." In this passage, we see Jesus' true intent about what it means to be born again. We are not born again in the flesh through reincarnation, but of the Spirit when we accept Jesus Christ as our Lord and Savior. Through water baptism, we give a public display of dying to our old selves as we are submerged our sins our flung into the depths and as we emerge new life is imbued into us. Before baptism, we confess our sins by stating to God, "Lord, please forgive me of my sins. I believe you died for me on the cross for the forgiveness on my and all of humanity's sins if only they will hear and accept it. You died and were risen on the 3$^{rd}$ day. I turn from my old ways and follow you from this day forward. I make you my Lord and Savior, amen!" In this way, we receive the Holy Spirit, something that cannot be seen but can most definitely be felt. As Jesus describes, it is akin to the wind that can be felt on our skin; we don't see it but nonetheless we can experience and know that it exists. Through prayer and praise to God, we can feel this presence that fills out bodies with light and positive energy. You might not see it, but you can feels it presence, like the wind caressing the skin.

Now returning to our original refutation, is our body a soul trap? No, it is instead something that should be honored and taken care, the vehicle to fulfill our creative purpose here on earth; that which we have been give stewardship over during our existence. The Bible describes it as a temple or sanctuary, something quite different from what the Gnostics view it as, a tomb or prison. Paul describes it succinctly in 1 Corinthians 6:19 when he writes about avoiding sexual immorality where it states, [19]"Do you now know that your body is a sanctuary of the Holy Spirit who is in you, whom you have from God? You are not your own, [20] for you were brought at a price; therefore, glorify God in your body." Our bodies are described as Holy Sanctuaries that have purpose here on earth. We are here to find that purpose and to also honor the body that God has given us. If the body is a sanctuary, it is not a soul trap.

In conclusion, God's plan for us here on earth is for us to create and fulfill the purpose for which we were created. Each one of us is created for a purpose here on earth that for which our Holy Sanctuaries or bodies were created. We are sent here to find and fulfill that purpose. That does not mean that we are given absolute freedom here on earth, but rather we must operate within the guardrails that God has defined for our existence, one that creates instead of one that causes decay and destroys. Jesus applicably describes it in the HSCB in John 15:5, "I am the vine; you are the branches. The one who remains in Me and I in him produces much fruit, because you can do nothing without Me." We remain in Jesus by following his Word and example for us as exhibited in the Bible. In doing so, we bring to fruition his final or ultimate Platonic cause, we are to love God above all else and love our neighbors.

## Notes and Sources

Essay 3

1. Barnstone, Willis. *The Other Bible.* HarperCollins Publishers, 1984, pgs 55, 56, 58.
2. Meyer, Marvin. *The Nag Hammadi Scriptures – The Revised and Updated Translation of Sacred Gnostic Texts.* HarperOne, 2007, pgs 84, 85, 86, 96, 119.
3. Figures 1 & 2: Canva. Text-to-Image Generator. Accessed July 5, 2025. https://www.canva.com/
4. Several references were made to Holman Bible Publishers. *The Apologetics Study Bible: Holtman Christian Standard Bible (HCSB).* Nashville, TN: Holtman Bible Publishers, 2007.

www.ingramcontent.com/pod-product-compliance
Lightning Source LLC
Chambersburg PA
CBHW070457050426
42449CB00012B/3019